The Pine

Stories by Thich Nhat Hanh

Translated by
Vo-Dinh Mai & Mobi Ho

Illustrations by Vo-Dinh Mai

White Pine Press

ISBN 0-934834-27-X

Acknowledgements:

The stories "The Pine Gate" and "The Giant Pines" were translated by Vo-Dinh Mai. The story "The Ancient Tree" was translated by Mobi Ho in collaboration with the author. Special thanks to Arnie Kotler and Sister Phuong for their assistance.

The publication of this book was made possible, in part, by a grant from the New York State Council on the Arts.

Design by Watershed Design.

WHITE PINE PRESS
76 Center Street
Fredonia, New York 14063

Contents

The Pine Gate

1988

It was a cool, almost chilly, autumn evening, and the moon had just risen, when the young swordsman arrived at the foot of the mountain. The wilderness was bathed in the light of the full moon glimmering playfully on branches and leaves. It seemed to him that during the seven years he was away, nothing in the surroundings had changed. Nothing had changed, and yet nothing seemed to be greeting him with any warmth—he who had once lived there for years, and who was now returning from afar.

The swordsman paused at the foot of the mountain and looked up. Above him, the narrow path was barred by a pine gate which was tightly shut. He pushed at the gate's sturdy doors, but these remained immovable under his powerful hands.

He was puzzled. Never, as far back as he could remember, had his Master had the gate closed and locked like this. Since this was the only way up the mountain, he had no choice. Slapping the handle of his sword, he rose swiftly from the ground. But that was all. A strange force gripped his whole body and pushed it back down; he could not jump over the low gate. In a moment, he had unsheathed his long sword, but the sharp blade bounced back from the soft pine wood as if the latter were steel. The impact was so powerful it sent a shock through his hand and wrist. He raised his sword and examined its gleaming edge under the moonlight. The gate was indeed too hard; most certainly his Master had endowed it with the strength of his own spirit. It was closed, and no one was to pass. That was the way his Master wanted it. The swordsman sighed deeply. He returned his sword to it's sheath, and sat down on a big rock outside the gate.

Seven years earlier on the day he was to leave the mountain, his Master looked at him for a long moment without speaking. There was a kind expression in his eyes and something else, too, something that resembled pity. He could only bow his head in silence when his eyes encountered the compassionate and tolerant eyes of his Master. A while later, the old man said to him, "I cannot keep you at my side forever. Sooner or later, you must go down the mountain and into the world where you will have many opportunities in which to carry out the Way and to help people. I thought that perhaps I could keep you here with me a little longer, but if it's your will to go, my child, then go in peace. There is only this: Remember, always, what I have taught you and given to you, always. Down in the world below this mountain, you will need all of it."

Then his Master went over briefly again what he was to avoid, seek, leave alone, and change. Finally, he put a gentle hand on his shoulder: "Those are the yardsticks for your actions. Never do anything that could cause suffering either to yourself or to others, in the present or in the future. And go without fear on the road which you believe will lead you and others to total enlightenment. Remember, always, the standards by which happiness and suffering, illusion and liberation must be measured. Without them, you would betray the Way itself, let alone help the world!

"I have already given you my precious sword. Use it to subdue monsters and devils. But I want you to look upon it more like a sharp blade that comes from your own heart with which you will subjugate your own ambitions and desires. Now, I have this for you, too, and this will make your task easier." Then his Master pulled out of his wide sleeve a small viewing glass, and handed it to him.

"This is the Me Ngo glass," he said. It will help you to determine good and evil, to separate the virtuous from the wicked. It is also called the Demon Viewer, for looking through it, you will see the true forms of demons, evil spirits, and the like..."

He received the fabulous viewing glass from his Master's hand, but he was so grateful and so deeply moved he could not say one word. The following day, at the break of dawn, he went up to the central hall to take leave of his old Master. The old man walked down the mountain with him, all the way to Tiger Brook, and there, in the murmuring of a mountain stream, master and disciple bade farewell. His Master again put a hand on his shoulder and looked into his eyes. He went on looking as the young man started walking away. Once more, he called after his disciple, "Remember, my child, poverty cannot weaken you, wealth cannot seduce you, power cannot vanquish you. I will be here for the day you come back, your vows fulfilled!"

He recalled the first days of his journey vividly. Then, months, and years went through his mind. How humanity had revealed itself to him under different guises! And how helpful the sword and the Me Ngo viewing glass had been to him! Once, he met a priest whose appearance instantly inspired reverence, who—such an honor for the young swordsman—invited him back to his retreat where they would, in the words of the old sage, "discuss how best to join their efforts for the purpose of helping their fellow human beings." At first, the young man listened with rapture, but then, something odd about the priest struck him. He whipped out the Me Ngo and looked through it. In front of him, there was a gigantic demon! Its blue eyes sent forth crackling sparks, a horn stood out from its forehead, and its fangs were as long as his own arms! In one jump, the young man backed away, drew his sword, and furiously attacked it. The demon fought back but, of course, had no chance. It prostrated itself at the young man's foot, begging for mercy. The swordsman then demanded that it swear, under oath, it would return where it had come from, to study the Way, pray that one day it would be permitted to come back into the world of men as a true human being, and refrain from ever disguising itself again as a priest to bewitch and devour the innocent. Another time, he met a mandarin, an old man with a long white beard. It was a happy encounter between a young hero out to save the world and a high official, a "father and mother to the people," bent on finding better and better ways to govern and benefit the masses. Again, the young man's instinct was aroused: under the Me Ngo, the handsome, awe-inspiring old official turned out to be an enormous hog whose eyes literally dripped with greed. In one instant, the sword flew out of its sheath. The hog tried to flee, but the swordsman, in one jump, overtook it. Standing astride the main threshold of the mandarin's mansion, he barred the only escape route. The beast took on its true form and cried out loudly for mercy. Again, the young man did not leave the monster without extracting from it the solemn oath that it would follow the Way, that it would never again take the form of a mandarin so that it could gnaw the flesh and suck the blood of the people.

And there was that time, walking by a marketplace, when he saw a crowd surrounding a bookstall. The picture-and-book seller was a very beautiful young woman whose smile was like an opening flower. Seated nearby was another young woman, also of stunning beauty, who was singing softly some melodious tunes while plucking the strings of a lute. The beauty of the girls and the grace of the songs so captivated everyone present that no one left the stall once they had stopped, and all anyone could do was stand and listen, enraptured, and buy the pictures and books. The young man himself was attracted by the scene. He finally approached and held up one of the pictures. The elegance of the design and vividness of the colors overwhelmed him. Yet, an uneasiness rose within him. He reached for his Me Ngo. The two beautiful girls were actually two enormous snakes whose tongues darted forth and back like knife blades. The swordsman swept everyone aside in one movement of his arms, and with his sword pointing at the monsters, he shouted like thunder, "Demons! Back to your evil nature!"

The crowd scattered in fright. The big snakes swung at the young man, but no sooner did the fabulous sword draw a few flashing circles around their bodies than the reptiles coiled at his feet in submission. He forced their jaws open and carved out their venom-filled fangs with his sword. Then he put the bookstall to the torch and sent the monsters back to their lairs with the solemn promise, against certain total destruction, that they would never come back to bewitch the village people.

So, the young swordsman went on from village to village, and from town to town, on a mission he had set for himself, using the weapon and the viewing glass his Master had given him, along with priceless counsels. He threw himself into his task. For a time now he had come to think of himself as The Indispensable Swordsman. The world could not do without his presence. He had come down from the mountain into the world, and he participated fully in the life down here. Facing the world where treachery and cunning reigned he had to learn flexibility and patience, and at times he had to bend with the tide because his goal was to vanquish and to persuade. He experienced great pleasure in his actions for the good. He went so far as to reach the point where he forgot to eat and sleep. And he did more, much more, because of the joy and satisfaction he derived from the pursuit of his goal—helping the people—rather than because of this goal itself. He served because that fulfilled him, not necessarily because the people needed him.

And so, seven years passed. One day, as he was resting on the bank of a river, watching the water flow by quietly, he suddenly realized that for some time now he had not used the Me Ngo viewing glass. He had not used it, he was now aware, not because he had forgotten that he had it, but because he had not felt like using it. Then, he remembered that there had been times when he did use the glass, but only very reluctantly. Those days when he first came down from the mountain, he fought to the death every time he saw, through the Me Ngo, the true natures of whatever evil faced him. He recalled his great happiness each time, through the glass, he saw the image of a virtuous man or a true sage. But, obviously, something odd had happened to him recently, and he did not know what. It seemed to him he began to feel no great joy when he saw wisemen in his viewing glass, just as he felt no great fury when he saw in it the images of monsters and devils. When monsters appeared in his miraculous glass, the young swordsman couldn't help noticing that there happened to be a certain familiarity even in their horrifying inhuman features.

The Me Ngo remained safely in his pocket, even though it had not been used for a long time. Then the young swordsman thought he would return some day to the mountain to ask his Master's advice: why did he have such reluctance to use what obviously had been such a great help to him? But only on the twelfth day of the eighth month, while he was crossing a forest of white plum trees and was struck by the snow-white blossoms gleaming under the autumn moon, did he suddenly yearn for the days when he studied as a young man under his old Master, whose cottage stood at the border of just such an old plum forest. Only then did he decide to return. In his wish to see his Master, the journey back seemed interminable: seven days and seven nights of climbing hills and crossing streams. But as he reached the foot of the high mountain where he would begin the ascent to his Master's abode, darkness descended. The rising moon showed the two leaves of the heavy pine gate shut tightly, preventing him from going any further up the mountain.

There was nothing he could do but wait. At dawn, he thought, one of his "brothers" would certainly come down to fetch water from the stream and could open the gate for him. By now, the moon had risen past its zenith. The entire mountain and forest were bathed in its cool light.

As the night wore on, the air became chillier. He pulled out his sword and watched the moon gleam on its cold, sharp edge. Then he sheathed it again and stood up. The moon seemed extraordinarily bright. The mountain, the forest, everywhere—all was still, and quiet, as if the world was oblivious to his presence. Feeling dejected, he dropped down onto another rock. Again, the seven years of his recent life passed before him. Slowly, ever slowly, the moon edged towards the distant summit of a far mountain. In the sky, the stars shone brightly but then they, too, began to recede, becoming paler and paler. There was already the hint of a glow in the east. The outlines of the mountain became suddenly sharper against the pale sky. Dawn was about to break.

There was rustling of dry leaves. The swordsman looked up and saw the vague form of someone walking down the mountain. He thought it must be one of his younger "brothers," though it was not light enough and the figure was too distant for him to make out the latter's features. It must be a "brother" because the person was carrying something like a large pitcher. Whoever it was came closer and closer, and the swordsman heard him exclaim happily:

—Elder Brother!

—Younger Brother!

—When did you arrive? Just now?

—No! As a matter of fact, I arrived here when the moon was just coming up! I've waited all night down here. Why, in Heaven's name, did anyone lock up the gate like this? Was it the Master's order?

The younger disciple, smiling, raised his hand and pulled, ever so lightly, at the heavy gate. It swung open with ease. He stepped outside it, and, grasping the swordsman's hands in his own, looked at his senior:

—You must be chilled to the bones staying down here

all night. You're covered with dew! Well, I used to come down here all day, picking herbs and watching the gate, you know.... If I thought someone deserved an audience with the Master, I'd bring him up, and if I didn't, I'd just make myself invisible! I'd just stay behind the bushes, and they'd just give up! You know that our Master doesn't want to see anyone unless he has a true determination to learn. Lately, the Master has allowed me to move on to further studies, and as I stay most of the time up at the retreat he told me to close the gate. He told me it would open itself for virtuous people but would stay shut and bar the way for those too heavy with the dust of the world! There is no way anyone could ever climb it or jump over it. Especially someone burdened with the spirits of demons and the like! The swordsman knitted his brows:

—Would you say I am such a person? Would you? Why did the gate stay shut for me?

The younger man laughed heartily:

—But of course not! How could you be such a person? Anyway, we can go up now, you see that the way is clear. But just a moment, Elder Brother! I must fetch some water first. Come with me. Smile, Brother, smile! Who are you angry at?

Both men laughed. They made their way down to the stream. The sun was not yet up, but the east already glowed brightly. The two disciples could now see clearly each line on the other's face. The water was tinted a pale rose by the dawn. There, they could see their reflections next to one another. The swordsman was bold and strong in his knight's suit; a long sword slung diagonally over his back. The younger disciple's figure was gentler in his flowing page's robe, a pitcher in his hands. Without speaking, both looked at their own reflections, and smiled to one another. A water-spider sprung up suddenly and caused the rose-tinted surface to ripple, sending the images into thousands of undulating patterns.

—How beautiful! I would certainly destroy our reflections for good if I dipped the pitcher in now. By the way, do you still have the Me Ngo viewing glass with you? Master gave it to you when you came down the mountains years ago!

The swordsman realized that it was true, that all these years he had used it only to look at others, but never once had he looked at his own image. He took the glass out, wiped it on his sleeve, then pointed it at the water's surface. The two heads came close to look through the small glass together.

A loud scream escaped from the throat of the two young men. It reverberated through the forest. The swordsman fell forward and collapsed on the bank of the stream. A deer, drinking water further upstream, looked up in fright.

The younger disciple could not believe what he had seen in the glass; there he was in his flowing robe, a pitcher in hand, standing next to a towering demon with eyes deep and dark like waterwells and long fangs curving down around its square jaw. Yes, he saw the color of the demon's face. It was a bluish gray, the shade of ashes and death. The young man shuddered, and rubbing his eyes, looked again at his senior who was now lying unconscious on the blue stones of the bank. The older man's face still expressed shock and horror; suffering had been etched upon this man who, for seven years, had ceaselessly braved the rough and cruel world down below their mountain retreat.

The young disciple rushed down to the stream to fetch water and to douse his elder's face with it. Moments later, the swordsman came to. His face was ravaged with despair. His true image had appeared in the Me Ngo so unexpectedly, bringing self-knowledge to him in such a swift, brutal fashion that he could do nothing but collapse under this blow. All his energy seemed to have left him. He tried to stand up, but there was no strength in his legs and arms.

—It's all right, it's all right, my brother! We'll go up now.

To the swordsman's ears, his brother's voice was like an imperceptible movement of the breeze, a faint murmur from afar. He shook his head. His world had collapsed, and he wanted to live no longer. He felt as if his body and soul had been in the path of a hurricane. He could not possibly entertain the idea, the affront, of bringing himself, ever, into his beloved Master's presence.

The younger man brushed some sand off his brother's shoulder:

—No, you shouldn't worry about it. You know that the Master had nothing but compassion for you. Let's go up now. We'll again live and work and study together...

Up the steep, rock-strewn path snaking up the mountain, the two figures made their way slowly. It was not, as yet, day; the silhouettes imprinted themselves on the thin veil of dew stretching over trees and rocks. The first sun rays finally reached the two men and heightened the contrast: the swordsman only seemed more broken in both body and spirit, walking next to the younger disciple whose steps were firm and whose mien gentle.

And over the mountain top, far away, the sun rose.

Nhat Hanh

Notes

In the Far East (China, Japan, Korea, Vietnam) there was an old tradition demanding that wise old men (Taoist monks or Buddhist priests) retired to mountain tops, built retreats—usually called "stone grottoes" or "grass huts"—accepted a few selected disciples, and taught them the

"Way." In addition to spiritual studies, the martial arts with a non-violent approach were given great importance. The arts of the sword, the staff, Yoga, Judo, Karate, Kung-fu, etc. were taught by the old Masters who later would send their disciples down into the world. Disciples were ranked either by the order in which they had been accepted by their Masters, by age, or by abilities. They called one another "Elder Brother" or "Younger Brother". The "gurus" were called su-phu, literally: Master-Father.

THE GIANT PINES

After striking the great bronze temple bell one hundred and seven times, the novice Tam-The of Phap-Van Temple turned the big wooden mallet around and with it knocked gently twice on the bell's spine: a warning to his elder fellow-novice Tam-Hien that after one more strike the bell rituals would be complete and the dawn ceremony would begin. He waited patiently until the last vibrations from the one-hundred-and-seventh stroke died away before he raised the mallet and struck the one-hundred and eighth.

From a corner of the temple, the sound of Tam-Hien's "gong" reached his ears. Tam-The answered the first three strikes with three new strikes of his own on the great bell, then laid the mallet down to rest while Tam-Hien's three rolls of the gong went on. The monks were all assembled at the main hall and ready for the morning devotional.

Tam-The put his palm-leafed raincoat over his shoulders—the air was chilly—descended from the bell tower, and went out its door. The morning mist was still thick. Swiftly, he made his way toward the main gate of the temple where the wandering monk had taken shelter overnight.

His guest had arrived in the afternoon the day before but had declined his offer of bed and board in the temple and asked only to be permitted to rest outside. His only request had been for a straw mat to lie on under the roof of the gate. He insisted that was all he needed, for as soon as the mist cleared in the morning he would be gone. His brown monk's robe, already very worn and faded, was thick with dust from the journey. Instead of being clean-shaven as a monk should be, his hair and beard were long and unkempt. His face, hands, and feet were filthy, and from his person rose a sour, awful stench. Tam-The had gone back in to fetch a basin of water and a handtowel. He left again and returned with a straw mat which he spread on the stone steps of the great gate. He waited until the traveller had done his washing so he could take the basin of dirty water away, then returned once more with a small wooden tray on which he had placed a bowl of rice gruel, some pickled mustard greens, a small dish of soybean sauce, and a pair of chopsticks. The old monk thanked him, and in a most leisurely fashion began to eat. Tam-The clasped his hands together in respectful greetings and went back in. About an hour later, returning to the gate, he saw that the traveller had already wrapped himself in the straw mat and was fast asleep. He bent down to pick up the tray with both hands and, noiselessly, made his way back to the temple's kitchen.

The next morning, going to the gate again, Tam-The found his guest sitting in deep meditation. He was not sitting in the lotus position; his right knee was up to his chest with his right foot placed flat on the ground. Tam-The noticed that the horrible stench arising from the monk was still there, yet he was struck by his noble bearing. He was about forty-five or fifty, and although half-hidden by overgrown hair and beard, his face had a clarity, a distinction, that was awe-inspiring. "This must be one of those mysterious monks one hears about," Tam-The thought, "the monk didn't want to impose his terrible appearance on us. If I talk to him a little, perhaps I will learn something about him." Tam-The was about to go back for a basin of warm water for his guest when the latter opened his eyes. Tam-The clasped his hands and bowed. The old monk cleared his throat and gently said:

"Pray, Respected Novice, tell me, how far is it now from here to Cuu-Lung Mountain?"

Tam-The replied with great humbleness:

"Most Venerable, it's not far, only about half-a-day's walk. I would like to go and bring you a basin of warm water for your morning wash."

The traveller raised a hand to indicate it was not necessary. He leaned back against the wall, and pushing against it, raised himself with difficulty. Then he reached out for his bamboo stick.

"Thank you all the same, Young Monk. I must go now if I want to arrive before dark."

No sooner had he said it then he started limping away, stick in hand. Tam-The started walking, too, with the intention of seeing him off downhill all the way to where the mountain road branched off in two directions, but the stranger again raised his hand to tell him not to bother.

Hobbling and limping, he was off.

"I can't see how he can make it to Cuu-Lung Mountain in good time," Tam-The shook his head in sympathy. "Going such a long way and without even a small bag! So thin, too; all skin and bones, and covered with dust and dirt. Why in the world does he want to go to Cuu-Lung in such a hurry?"

All these years he had never heard of any temple or tower over on Cuu-Lung Mountain. He had never even seen the mountain itself. All he knew was that Cuu-Lung was high and wild, its summit perpetually hidden in mist and clouds. He realized that he had come to like the old stranger very much, a liking full of sympathy and respect. There was something about the monk that made Tam-The wish he could know him better, even to be near him. But now he was gone. Tam-The knew nothing about him the evening before, and now he knew nothing more, except that the old monk was leaning on his bamboo stick and limping along the mountain road towards Cuu-Lung. There was nothing for him to do but walk back to his temple and, with the help of other young novices, get some bowls of rice gruel ready for the monks' breakfasts. The morning devotional will be coming to an end soon, he thought.

The old monk made his way slowly, with much difficulty, because, on his left thigh, there was an enormous boil about the size of a grapefruit. The boil gave him terrible pain, but only when he slept did he sometimes moan softly. After being told by the young novice that just half-a-day's walk remained between him and Cuu-Lung Mountain, he had hoped that by starting early he would at least reach its foot by nightfall. But the boil hurt so much he was not covering much ground and he had to spend that night under a tree. That he had no food at all was no great problem: the six months he had been on the road there had been countless times he slept under a tree with not a grain of rice in his stomach. If, at nightfall, there was a pagoda nearby, he would knock and ask for permission to sleep under its gates. A young novice—just like Tam-The—would bring a bowl of gruel or rice and offer it to him as was the custom. He recalled, in particular, the novice he had met the night before—such thoughtfulness, such kindness! He had even brought him a basin of warm water and a straw mat, obviously freshly washed for it still smelled of the good sun. But this night, all he had was a great big tree root to put his head on. He wanted to sleep, but the high mountain air was so chilly he had to curl up to keep warm, and even then he was so cold he hardly slept at all through the night.

It was not yet daylight when the traveller again got to his feet to continue his journey. He was so weak he fell down several times; once he thought he was not going to be able to get up again, but he went on. A few hundred steps later, he stopped and sat down on a rock. As soon as his normal breathing returned, he reached for his bamboo stick and, leaning on it, started off. So he continued on until the Hour of The Monkey when he finally reached the foot of Cuu-Lung.

He stood at the foot of the mountain and looked around. He saw no signs of human presence. He looked as far as he could see for a pale grey strand of smoke which would indicate that, far away, someone, perhaps in the home of a woodcutter, was boiling rice for the evening meal. He couldn't even see the outline of the summit above, for it was shrouded in thick mist. How was he to find the "grass hut" of the person he wanted to see? The old monk sat down to rest on a large,, jutting stone. There he was, after six months of dragging himself towards Cuu-Lung Mountain. It's a strange coincidence, he thought to himself, remembering suddenly those verses from the ancient Chinese poet Gia-Dao:

> My friend, for years past, has lived here, at this mountain,
> But in this thick cloud and mist, how can I ever find him?

Sixteen years earlier, the old traveller, who was then Tri-Huyen, a young man studying for the priesthood, had met an Indian monk at an old temple in the capital city. The Indian, whose name was Kaniska, was covered with foul-smelling sores. When he stopped at the temple to ask for temporary shelter, everyone was overwhelmed by disgust. Tri-Huyen alone did not mind; he took good care of the stranger. Every morning, he brought a basin of hot water to Kaniska's room. Having diluted a fistful of seasalt in it, he helped the Indian monk bathe himself. Afterwards, he would bring a freshly laundered robe for him to change into, and he would take away the one soaked with pus and blood to wash and hang in the sun. At noon, Tri-Huyen would bring his rice. In the evening, he would carry hot tea to him and take away the dirty dishes. Though Kaniska's illness did not seem to abate, with time the care Tri-Huyen was giving him brought him much comfort. For two long years, Tri-Huyen cared for Kaniska as if he were a brother. His patience was steady and his thoughtfulness constant, everyday, for two years. Fortunately, Tri-Huyen's superiors never said a word of disapproval to him: he was given tacit permission to care for the stranger because, at the same time, never once did Tri-Huyen neglect his own studies and other temple responsibilities.

One morning, after having been helped with his painful

bathing and dressing, the Indian monk said to Tri-Huyen's

"You have cared for me for a long time now. I am much indebted to you. But beginning tomorrow you will have to no longer, for I will be leaving this afternoon."

Tri-Huyen was completely taken aback:

"But, Most Venerable, where are you going? You are still quite ill. Who's going to care for you?"

Kaniska looked at him with infinite gentleness. Slowly, he replied:

"I have unfinished business, and it's time I go. Please, do not be concerned. There are temples on the way. Someone will surely be kind enough..."

The Indian monk, however, could see that the student's clear and peaceful face was clouded by sadness:

"Please, do not think of this as the end of our friendship. Our paths will cross again. I know for certain that you are in possession of a brilliant mind and that your studies will bear fruit. You will one day become a great monk and teacher. Your fame will spread far and wide. Let me only say this to you: the aim of studying the Way is to become free, not for any other gain, however desirable. We have known each other only for a short time, but our friendship is deep and true, so I think I may take the liberty of reminding you of this. Please, remember it."

Tri-Huyen bowed his head in acknowledgement and gratitude. Then, he asked:

"You said we will meet again... but pray, when? And where? I'm afraid that on your journey you will not leave behind even your footsteps."

"If it is our destiny to meet, then even if we try to run away from one another, we will still meet! Don't worry about such a thing! Just let me tell you that in this lifetime you will reach the pinnacle of your achievements and glories. But fourteen or fifteen years from now you will also meet your most terrible ordeal. Remember me then and come to me, and I will be able to help you."

"But then, how will I know where to find you?" Tri-Huyen asked. The Indian monk put a hand on Tri-Huyen's shoulder and lead him out of his monk's cell:

"You will come to Cuu-Lung Mountain, at Ban-Thanh District, in the Country of Tay-Thuc. You will stand at its foot and look up, and where you see two immense pine trees standing together, is where you will find me. Please, remember the names: Cuu-Lung Mountain. In Thuc country."

So the Indian left, and never again did Tri-Huyen hear his name mentioned. Time passed, and the young student became a full-fledged monk whose erudition, wisdom, and eloquence were recognized far and wide. Each time he preached, thousands came to hear him. The capital city was hardly short of great monks and teachers, but Tri-Huyen's reputation was such that even King Y-Tong was aware of it. That year, during the Lord Buddha's birthday celebrations, the king sent for him to come into the palace and preach to the royal family and the entire court. There he was, sitting on an elevated dais above all present, the picture of a living Buddha: his appearance was handsome, his bearing noble, his voice ringing and deep, and his words swept everyone off into the Marvelous World of the Dharma. The king was deeply pleased, and ordered that a purple monk's habit be offered up to him. From then on, the Venerable Tri-Huyen's fame spread even further and wider. Yet, he was still only forty-three. It came to be that after Tri-Huyen had given several such performances, His Majesty prostrated Himself one day in front of Tri--Huyen and proclaimed him to be the "Teacher of the Nation." By royal decree, the king bestowed upon the monk the glorious name of Ngo-Dat ("The One Who Has

Attained Enlightenment"). An-Quoc Temple, next door to the royal palace, was spruced and readied to become the Master's own Resident Temple; the king wanted him nearby so that he could see him often and easily and benefit from his teachings.

But all these honors paled next to what happened when the Great Teacher reached his forty-fifth birthday. On that special occasion, by royal proclamation, the entire populace sent their chosen representatives to the capital to hear the Great Teacher expound on the "Lotus Flower of the Wonderful Dharma" Sutra. Five thousand seats were set aside for the royal family, the court, and the best minds of the nation. The folks of the capital city arrived like an avalanche: people were standing in row after row, filling every available space within the temple courtyard. Thousands listened to the Great Teacher's voice rise and reverberate over them like the wind, like the waves. For an entire month the sermons continued, and, for the entire time, the king himself never missed attendance.

Then, the final session of the month-long event arrived. For this, the king had a special platform fashioned from fragrant cedar wood by the most skillful craftsmen of the realm. It was placed very high so that thousands of the faithful would be able to see him. The ceremony was conducted in utmost solemnity. The king stood, walked over to the Great Teacher, bowed to him, and invited him to step onto the magnificent platform. As the Most Venerable Ngo-Dat did so, the entire audience went down on its knees; many were so moved they wept. And so the final session began. It was to be one the Great Master and Teacher Ngo-Dat would never in his life forget for it brought about the most cataclysmic change in the entire spiritual existence of the one who had been the young monk Tri-Huyen.

Sitting now on a rock at the foot of Cuu-Lung Mountain, the emaciated wanderer recalled vividly the moment he sat down, with crossed legs, on the cedar platform the king had offered him. Below and all around him, thousands were bowing low, in awe—the king was among them. Ngo-Dat looked down, and even he was amazed. It was indeed extraordinary for a monk, one who had forsaken everything for the Way, to have reached such a lofty place among mortals. And so, for a moment, for the batting of an eye, he felt proud of his accomplishment. Yes, he felt pride in himself. Immediately, a strange fire surged to his face, and he knew that evil had penetrated him. He shook himself lightly and tried to regain control, but it was too late. From the distant sky, a minute and luminous object, like a brilliant grain of sand, hurled down and struck his left thigh, sending an excruciating pain through his flesh, deep into his bones and marrow. The pain was so terrible Ngo-Dat let out a cry and clasped his thigh in his hands. The king rose abruptly from his throne and shouted for attendants to help the Great Teacher down from his platform. Thus, what was to have been the last, glorious session of Ngo-Dat's preaching on the "Lotus Flower of the Wonderful Dharma" Sutra never took place: everyone thought that the Great Teacher had been bitten by some small poisonous creature, a centipede perhaps, for immediately afterwards, he began to run a high fever.

Ngo-Dat, alone, knew that no centipede had bitten him; he had seen that luminous particle from space flying straight down at him like lightning to penetrate his flesh without damaging the monk's habit that covered it. He knew, but he said nothing; he let the busy royal physicians go on with their theories and treatments. The small wound began to fester. It quickly became a swollen purple mass, as large as a grapefruit, and dreadfully painful. About ten days later, the swelling burst, turning into an enormous sore from which blood and pus poured out, enough each day to fill a large bowl. The royal physicians were busier than ever; they prescribed all manner of medication, some to be taken internally, some for external application. None, however, proved to be of any help. King Y-Tong, deeply concerned, went daily to pay his respects to his Teacher while ordering that all efforts must be made to find better physicians and better medicine. Yet, a year passed, and the Great Teacher's condition only worsened. He lost weight, and his strength just ebbed away. During one of his visits, the king believed he saw a tear trembling in the eye of the holy man.

One night, after spending painful, sleepless hours, Ngo-Dat reached a decision: he would leave the great temple, the king and the people he had made his own. For an entire year, he had lain there, waited on hand and foot by an army of physicians and attendants, without being of any use to the nation. He had reached the pinnacle of honor, and he now knew the bottomless pit of shame and torment. That very night, he stole away with only a simple brown monk's robe on his back and a staff, a gift from the king, in his hand. The sore was excruciating, but by tremendous effort he made his way through the night, out of the capital. When he happened to see a bamboo stick lying on the roadside, he picked it up; and crossing the first bridge, threw the royal cane down into the swift river. The precious staff floated away toward the capital while the former Teacher of the Nation, now a sick, desperate man, went on limping toward the mountains.

At noon the first day, the traveller passed through a rural marketplace. Seeing a monk in such pitiful condition, a peasant woman offered him two bananas and a handful of sweet rice. He feared, however, that the latter would make his sore worse, and accepted only the fruits. As he sat eating them, on a mound of earth, he realized that someone might recognize him; so he smeared his face with mud and dirt. Then, suddenly, while he was busy doing that, not knowing where to go and what to do next, the image of the old Indian monk came to his mind like a flash of lightning. He remembered what the holy Kaniska had told him years earlier: "In fourteen or fifteen years, you will meet the most terrible ordeal of your life. Come to me then, and I will help you... Come to Cuu-Lung Mountain, in Thuc Country...."

So, walking by day and resting by night, the wandering-monk Ngo-Dat set out for Thuc despite the pain in his body. Blood and pus continually soaked through his trousers, but he had no change of clothes. The foul-smelling secretions poured out and dried up again and again, and his trousers were now stiff like old corn stalks, the stench was overpowering. Even his monk's robe had become badly stained, both front and back. Where there were no stains, the original brown was so faded it was the color of dust. When evening came, he stopped to sit down on the big root of a tree or on a rock, and, pulling up a leg of his trousers, looked at the sore. It was big as a grapefruit, and its festering surface had four small openings that were brilliant crimson: the two low ones, nearest his knee, looked like eyes; the one in the middle like a nose; and the one on top flared out like an angry, bloody mouth. He looked at the sore as if looking at a human face. He and his own sore faced one another as if in a mute contest. It seemed that the sore was rolling its eyes and clenching its teeth at him in utter hatred and fury, but he could only stare back. He felt no anger, only sorrow and desolation. He knew he was looking at the curse he brought upon himself.

So, on his long journey to Thuc Country, the former Teacher of the Nation slept under many temple gates, but no one ever recognized him under the filth and stench. Everyone had been kind but none had been as kind as the young novice at Phap-Van Temple, who even brought him warm water and rice gruel. He remembered him with delight. And now, he was at the foot of Cuu-Lung Mountain.

The wandering-monk—a fortnight ago The Great Teacher of The Nation— flinched. He heard the murmuring of a nearby brook, and the words of the Indian monk Kaniska sprang to his mind: "Cuu-Lung Mountain... You will stand at its foot and look up, and where you see two immense pine trees, that's where you will find me...".

Ngo-Dat looked up, and there they were, the giant pines. On the left side of the mountain, high up, the mist had cleared: two great trees stood together in all their extraordinary rectitude and grandeur, their tops still hidden in clouds. Ngo-Dat reached for his bamboo stick: step by painful step, he felt his way up the left face of the mountain.

At times, he crawled on his belly for he was at the end of his strength and the big sore gave him great pain. But finally, he looked up and could hardly believe what he saw: half-hidden behind luxuriant vegetation were the multicolored and brilliant roofs and gates of a temple which, even at such distance, seemed to be of extraordinary beauty. From far away, the delicate sounds of a windbell reached him and he thought he was hearing the wind move the Tree of the Seven-Jewels as described in the Amitayus-Sutra. A bird's melodious singing sounded nearby; he thought it must be the sweet voice of the Karavinka bird. As he reached the three-portal main gate, he met a novice coming out from under it. He inquired and was told that this was indeed the temple where The Most Venerable Kaniska resided. The novice then went back in to announce the visitor, and a short moment later, Kaniska walked out. His old friend, resplendent like a Bodhisattva, was such a vision that Ngo-Dat fell down on his knees and prostrated himself in a deep, respectful greeting. Kaniska bent down, helped the former Teacher of the Nation to his feet, and, with a gentle hand, led him into the main reception hall of his temple.

There, between them, they emptied a small teapot which had a fragrance that all but awakened Ngo-Dat from the deep slumber of the past fifteen years. Kaniska began to question his friend about his recent life and work. Though he was already a man of forty-six and had been the most exalted Great Teacher of The Nation, Ngo-Dat could not help feeling as pitiful as a small, helpless child: in detail, he told his host everything. Kaniska listened intently, now and then sighing in sorrowful compassion for what his friend had been through. Then, he asked to see the sore. Ngo-Dat stood up, pulled up one leg of his trousers, and showed it to his friend. The sore was a terrible sight: it glared at the two men. Kaniska told his friend to take his seat again, and said:

"My friend, below this mountain there is a brook called The Brook That Unties The Bind. Its water can help rid you of this monstrous sore. You will stay here tonight; the first thing in the morning, we'll go down together, and I myself will help you wash. The sore will go away, I assure you. Two washings will do it, my friend."

Then the Most Venerable Kaniska left for a moment and returned with a basin of warm water and a bowl of salt, and, smiling, said:

"Honored Friend, long ago you washed this pitiful body of mine for two years, do you remember? Now, before the water of the miraculous brook does its work, allow me the joy of cleaning your sore for you. For the last time..."

Out of respect, Ngo-Dat was about to decline his friend's offer, but glancing up, he met Kaniska's eyes and knew it was no use. Kneeling on the floor, and in the most solemn fashion, Kaniska poured water and washed Ngo-Dat's festering, foul-smelling sore. With only salted, warm water and a handcloth, Kaniska soothed away the loneliness and pain six months of wandering had inflicted upon his friend. Ngo-Dat watched his friend and was so moved by gratitude his eyes welled up with tears. When Kaniska finished, he left with the dirty basin and returned again with clean water and another towel. He took Ngo-Dat's robe off and began to bathe him. Then he told him to take off all his clothes again and washed his entire body from head to toe, as if the former Teacher of The Nation were a small child. Then he went away and came back with a clean monastic robe and helped his friend dress. All Ngo-Dat could do was let himself be cared for. The clean robe, still smelling of the sun, was light and soothing, and from it the fragrance of cedar wood arose and filled his nostrils. That evening, Ngo-Dat ate white rice gruel cooked and served by the Most Venerable himself. Then he was taken to a small, empty room with a clean-smelling cot. Kaniska bade him goodnight and they agreed that, after tea, they would go down to the brook early the next morning.

Some time past midnight, hearing the first striking of the bell, Ngo-Dat could wait no longer. All night, the sore had been hurting him worse than ever. It was a long way until morning. He remembered that he heard, as he arrived at the foot of the mountain, the murmurings of a brook, so he rose from his cot, put on his robe, and stole out of his cell.

The mist was thick and Ngo-Dat could hardly see his

way but he managed to find the path down. After limping for another distance, he again heard the brook. Finally, he found it.

He knelt down on a rock and pulled the left leg of his trousers up, exposing the sore. Breathing slowly and deeply, he brought himself to a state of deepest concentration. Mentally he recited the Name of the Lord Buddha, then bent over and scooped up the water with both hands. The water was so cold it stung his hands, and he spilled at least half of it. But the little that remained in the palm of his hand was enough. When it came in contact with the open sore, it gave him such a shock, such a stabbing pain, a pain that went straight to his marrow, that he fainted and collapsed on the bank of the brook. Although unconscious, he saw an angry, red face; its hair and beard upright, and it glared at him, and said:

"Ah! You! You who are reputed to be wise and well-read, tell me, have you ever read the Book of the Western Han?"

Though taken by complete surprise, Ngo-Dat maintained his composure and replied:

"Yes, I have."

"You have! Then you must recall the affair of Vien-An and Trieu-Pho, don't you? Because of Vien-An's slanderous statements Trieu-Pho had to die by back-chopping in the middle of the Eastern Market. Do you recall that? What a horror! What an injustice! Now, look at me: I am Trieu-Pho, and you, you are no one but Vien-An, the slanderer, the murderer! You have done me a terrible wrong. And for many lives now I have pursued you to make you pay for your crime. In ten consecutive existences on earth, I have hounded you, but I have been able to do nothing to you because in each existence you have been a great monk, even a saint, and your ways and conduct have been so blameless I could find no opening for an attack. But

Vien-An, I have now caught up with you! You have finally failed to keep yourself on the straight and narrow path. The king's devotion and the people's worship have brought you down: you have exposed yourself to pride and egotism. So here I am: I am this sore you are carrying on your body! I am your own curse and malediction!"

The former Teacher of The Nation looked straight at his interlocutor, at the hirsute, angry red face, and he broke out in a cold sweat. He was about to say something, but he knew there was really nothing to say and remained silent. He saw that the red face seemed to have become more subdued. Now it spoke with a less wrathful tone of voice:

"No, of course, you don't have to say anything. In so many existences I have myself suffered because of this desire for revenge, I myself have sunk in darkness because of my hatred for you. But the Most Venerable Kaniska has used the miraculous water to wash your sore, and in doing so, has washed away this hatred. I will no longer be after you. And you, it is your great blessing to have met the holy Kaniska and, today, to be saved by him. From now on we are no longer in debt to one another. Please, get some water and wash yourself once more! Hurry!"

Ngo-Dat woke suddenly, and sat bolt upright. He knelt down on a large rock and bent over the brook. He splashed two handfuls of water onto the big sore, and the pain was even more terrible than the first time, and he again lost consciousness. But this time, he no longer saw the angry red face. He only felt, in both his body and soul, a great peace descend. He saw he was in a deep forest, running, jumping over rocks and bushes with speed and agility as if he had wings, with the ease of a butterfly fluttering over the grass. He was a child running in a spring field, thick with yellow and purple wildflowers. Then, he was lying on his back on the surface of a river; he looked up and saw an immense blue sky. Now he was a child, clad in the New Year's clothes, running, frolicking on a snow-covered hillside. The child felt cold at last and ran inside to warm his little hands over a fire, and the child saw his grandmother sitting with her sewing basket. On the right of the fire was his mother, who looked at him with eyes flowing with tenderness. The hearth was so comforting he did not want to go out into the cold again. Then, suddenly, he heard the howlings of monkeys nearby.

Ngo-Dat awakened, and found himself still lying on the bank of the brook. All around him the forest was full of birds singing. The sun had risen and was now warming everything it touched. Ngo-Dat, too, felt warm and contented. He rose swiftly and pulled up the left leg of his trousers. The big sore was no longer red; its face was drier and not as deep, its skin firmer. The sore was healing.

Ngo-Dat stood up and felt so full of energy, he no longer needed his bamboo stick. He cast his eyes around for the path leading up to the mountain temple. He wanted to go up and thank his friend Kaniska, but no path was in sight. He was puzzled, for it was the path that brought him down to the brook during the night. No, there was no path, no walkway anywhere; there were only stones and bushes. He spotted a large rock nearby. It was the one on which he rested yesterday in the late afternoon when he first arrived at the foot of the mountain. He looked up. The sun had chased away all the mist, but he saw no roofs, no gate. Even the two immense pine trees, so tall their tops were hidden in clouds, had vanished. Everything that happened the day before seemed now like a dream to him. He sat down on the rock and thought back to those events: the tall trees, the discovery of the magnificent temples, the meeting with a young novice, his reunion with his friend Kaniska... He recalled the fragrant cups of tea that rid him of so much weariness, the washing by Kaniska, the cedar-scented monastic robe... He looked down at himself. He saw that he was still dressed in the same old, torn, foul-smelling clothes he had put on to start his journey six months before.

Ngo-Dat sighed deeply; he knew then what had actually happened, and he realized that the course of destiny had come full circle. He turned his face to the mountain, and bowed three times, his heart overflowing with gratitude, a gratitude laced with regret for he knew he would never again see his friend, the holy Kaniska.

The Venerable Tam-The, Patriarch of Phap-Van Temple, accompanied by two disciples, arrived at Chi-Duc on a sunny early afternoon. Chi-Duc was only a small "grass meditation hut" at the foot of Cuu-Lung Mountain, but its location was unusually beautiful. As they reached its vicinity, the master of the realm, a gentle monk just over forty years of age and bearing the Dharma name of Tin-Co, was already on the small bridge straddling the brook to greet them. The pine trees in the area were the kind that were not too thick in their foliage, but they were straight-bodied pines, all reaching up to heaven in complete uprightness. For a long time the Patriarch of Phap-Van had been hearing about this small retreat in the Cuu-Lung Mountain and wanted to visit it, but only now had his wish finally been realized. He was pleased he had taken the journey: looking around, he was delighted by every tree, every rock, every leaf in sight. He raised his eyes to the summit of the mountain which was still covered in mists and vapors; he looked at the tall pine trees rising into space in all their splendor and nobility, and at the delightful small temple-retreat half-hidden by the greenery. He nodded silently, in approval and admiration.

No sooner had the host and his guest taken their proper seats than tea was brought up by a novice. The first pot of tea had hardly been drunk when the Venerable Tam--The noticed, lying on a small writing desk nearby, a bound volume that was obviously being filled in. The calligraphy was excellent, he thought to himself. He asked to see it, and what he read on its cover was: "Water of Charity: The Book of Repentance." Venerable Tam-The put the sutra down on the desk and was about to inquire about it when the abbot of Chi-Duc said to him:

"This is, Most Venerable, the text of a ritual governing a ritual of repentance that my Master himself has prepared. The world has not seen the likes of it for this is the first copy."

Still looking intently at the small volume, Venerable Tam-The said:

"May I assume that your Honored Master is the one who founded this very noble temple? What was his august name, pray, do be kind enough to tell me."

"Yes, you are right, indeed, Your Most Venerable. This humble abode, my Master built it himself about forty years ago. As long as he was alive, the place had no formal name. Only after his passing did I name it. Since I was very mindful of my great debt towards my Master, I chose the name of Chi-Duc Zen Retreat. At the time he came here, there was no settlement of any kind for miles around. Only years after he built a small meditation hut here did a handful of peasants and woodcutters start to arrive and build their own places."

Venerable Phap-Van interjected gently:

"I suppose when the Most Honored Master came here, you had been with him, as a small child, of course?"

Tin-Co shook his head:

"Oh, no, Most Venerable, my Master came to Cuu-Lung Mountain here all by himself. I was only a child of seven then. My father was one of those woodcutters I just spoke about. It was my great fortune that when his eyes fell upon me, I became his disciple. All my education, literary as well as religious, my Master gave to me. There is only one thing, if I may speak about it, and that is my Master used to compliment me on my calligraphy. But to this day, I believe that my Master's own brushwork is truly the work of the gods."

Abbot Tin-Co reached for a bound volume and gave it to Venerable Phap-Van. One look, and Phap-Van recognized that it was the original copy of "Water of Charity: The Book of Repentance," with Tin-Co's master's own calligraphy. The script was firm yet graceful, bold yet delicate, like a dance of phoenixes. He shook his head in utter delight.

"What beauty! Marvelous writing!"

Then he looked up and said:

"There is no doubt that this is a very precious work. I wonder, however, why Your Venerable has not inscribed the noble name of your Honored Master on its first page here, so that posterity would know about Him and pay Him homage?"

Tin-Co replied:

"My Master did not want his name on it. He came here and lived the life of a hermit, unknown and nameless. What would be the point of leaving his name on a page?"

Then, after a moment of silence, he continued:

"The day my Master came here, there was only wilderness. With his own hands, he built the retreat, cleared the bushes, planted beans and grew rice. As I learned later, all his life he had never before done such work. The day he arrived here, he sat on a rock on the bank of the brook;

he was in great pain, and there was no strength left in him."

While Tin-Co spoke, the image of the wandering monk of forty years earlier came back swiftly into the mind of the Patriarch of Phap-Van. Yes, he was then only Novice Tam-The, a sixteen-year-old. He saw again in his mind the old monk's solemn expression, his majestic bearing, his worn robe covered with dust and dirt, and, again, he smelled the awful stench. Tin-Co's Master had been the stranger who asked for permission to sleep under his temple gate. It was he who found this Chi-Duc Temple. The Venerable Phap-Van stood up and clasped his hands in front of his chest:

"Most Honored Host, Your Master once stopped by our humble temple and stayed overnight forty years ago. I myself had the honor of bringing him water to wash and rice gruel for his supper. I dare say that our two temples, Chi-Duc and Phap-Van are neighbors, for only half-a-day's walk separates us. Won't you, for the sake of that, allow me to know the noble name of your Master for whom, even after such a brief encounter, I have felt until this day a most profound attachment and veneration?"

Faced with such genuine and respectful sentiments, Tin-Co was moved to stand up, too, and it was his turn to bow low to his visitor:

"Please, I beg you to remain seated; I am not worthy of such honor. No, I will not keep the secret from you, Most Venerable. It's, however, quite late in the day, and you and your attendants would do well to spend the night here. We'll burn candles, and we'll continue our conversation. I promise I'll not keep any secret from you."

The night advanced, and though all their disciples had retired, the Abbot of Chi-Duc and the Patriarch of Phap-Van still sat facing one another. On the writing desk, two white candles burned in silence. The mountain outside was all stillness. After telling Phap-Van all he knew about his Master, from the first encounter while he was still a student-monk, with the Indian monk Kaniska to the time he had been "The Great Teacher of The Nation" in the capital city, to that night when he scooped water from the brook and splashed it on his sore, Tin-Co cleared his throat once more and went on:

"My Master was so grateful to the holy Kaniska for having delivered him from such mortal hatred, he made a vow then and there that he would remain on this mountain for the rest of his life. He broke branches with his bare hands and built a little hut. He hunted for edible greens and fruits, he drank water from the brook, and he spent all the remaining time in meditation. From the few woodcutters he encountered, he obtained seeds for beans and vegetables, a hoe and even a machete. I was told later that during that time, my Master was infinitely more at peace than when he had been the "Great Teacher of The Nation" in the capital.

"After I became his disciple, I enlarged the garden and the vegetable patch, and from then on we always raised enough food for ourselves. Whenever I had a little leisure time, I cut extra firewood and, through my brother who was then still at home, sold it at the marketplace. The proceeds were enough to buy ink, brushes, and paper for my own studies. Come to think of it, my Master, when he saw these implements, couldn't resist! He started again to write. He wrote a great deal, but 'Water of Charity: The Book of Repentance' was the first one that came from his brush in this mountain. He called it 'Water of Charity' in honor of the holy Kaniska, who had used the water from the brook to wash away a curse that had hounded him for ten existences... My Master often admonished me: 'To follow the Way is to seek enlightenment and liberation, not gain and fame.' How I understand this, knowing as I do of my Master's vicissitudes! But he often told me to keep whatever I knew about him to myself, so, in truth, I should have obeyed him.

"But tonight, I know I can no longer do this. I have not enough strength for it. Why? Is it because you yourself have met him, so for me, you are, forgive my brashness, Your Venerable, a friend? Or, perhaps, facing you now, am I feeling closer to my departed Master, so that through you I can see his presence? Now that I have spoken to you, I will never again feel the need to speak about this to anyone else. To have told you about my Master has been like having a weight lifted from my shoulders. I am grateful to you. It is quite late, I am afraid. Let me show you your quarters and wish you a very restful sleep. Tomorrow morning, I will take you to my Master's tomb. I am sure too you will want to examine the many works he has left us."

Lying straight on the small cot, the patriarch of Phap-Van Temple remained awake. He thought that by now heavy mist completely shrouded Cuu-Lung Mountain. "Are all living creatures of the mountain and valley still awake, too," he wondered, for the silence seemed so alive. "Forty years. What does that span of time mean? What have I done in those past forty years? Of course, I studied, I worked with my hands, sat in meditation, and explained the sutras and expounded on Dharma. I was a young novice of sixteen, and now I am the head of a large temple. And yet, for forty years I remained tied down at Phap-Van while so much water flowed away in this brook at the foot of this Cuu-Lung Mountain.

Suddenly, the young novice Tam-The that he had been forty years earlier came alive in him. Tears welled up in his eyes. "Yes, I had the chance to bring him a basin of warm water for his washing, but I did not have the privilege of kneeling down and washing his foul-smelling sore like the Holy Kaniska did." Novice Tam-The felt he no longer wanted to remain the patriarch of a great temple. Being patriarch meant that he had no opportunity to grow vegetables, to plant corn, and to cut firewood, and thus no chance to come to Cuu-Lung Mountain in time. How far was this mountain from his own temple? He reminded himself: half-a-day's walk. Yet, forty years had gone before he got there! "Too late, too late," he muttered. "What is there now but the murmurings of the brook." The Patriarch of Phap-Van Temple, no, Novice Tam-The cocked his ear and listened. Yes, he could hear a faint rustling of water, a rustling that became fainter and fainter, softer and softer.

As Phap-Van dozed off, he saw two pine trees rising up, immense, on the flank of Cuu-Lung Mountain, and he saw that their tops were shrouded in thick mist—two pines, two great pines, tall as the sky itself.

The Ancient Tree

In a deep forest in the highlands stood an ancient tree. No one knew how many thousands of years it had lived. Its trunk was so large that the armspans of 18 people could not embrace it; great roots pushed up through the ground and spread to a radius of 150 feet. The earth beneath the tree's shadow was unusually cool. Its bark was as hard as rock; if you pressed a fingernail against it, pain ran through your finger. Its branches held tens of thousands of nests, sheltering hundreds of thousands of birds, both large and small.

In the morning, when the sun rose, the first rays of light were like a conductor's baton, initiating a mighty symphony, the voices of thousands of birds, a symphony as majestic as the sun dawning behind the summit of the mountain. All the creatures of the mountain and forest arose, either on two feet or four, slowly, in wonder.

In the great tree there was one hole large as a grapefruit from Bien Hoa and 12 yards from the ground. In the hole lay a small brown egg. No one could say if a bird had brought the beautiful egg to the hole. Some thought the egg had not come from a living bird but had been forged by the sacred air of the forest and the life energy of the great tree.

Thirty years passed; the egg remained intact. Some nights, birds would be startled from their sleep by a cloud hovering over the hole and a brilliant light shining there, illuminating an entire corner of the forest. Finally, one night, under a full moon, the egg opened and a strange bird was born. The bird was very little; it gave a small chirp in the cold night. The moon was very bright; the stars were very bright. The tiny bird cried throughout the night. Its cry was neither tragic nor bold; it was a cry of surprise and strangeness. It cried until the sun appeared. The first rays of light opened the symphony; thousands of birds' voices broke forth. From that moment, the little bird cried no more.

It grew quickly. The nuts and grains mother birds brought to the hole were always plenty. Soon the hole in the tree became too small, and the bird had to find another place, much larger, in which to live. It now knew how to fly; it looked for its own food and gathered sticks of straw to cover the floor of its new nest. Strangely, although the egg had been brown, the bird was as white as snow. When it flew, its wingspan was vast, and it moved slowly and very quietly. Often it flew to far-away places where white waterfalls tumbled day and night like the majestic breath of the earth and sky.

Sometimes the bird did not return for several days. When it returned, it lay in its nest all day and night, thoughtfully and quietly. Its two eyes were very bright; they never lost the look of surprise they had from the beginning.

Now, in the ancient forest of Dai Lao, a hermit's small hut stood on the slope of a hill. There a monk had lived for almost 50 years. The bird often flew across Dai Lao forest; from time to time it saw the monk slowly walking down the path to the spring, holding a water jug in his hand. One day, smoke gently lingered over the roof of the humble hut and an atmosphere of warmth surrounded the hill. The bird saw two monks together on the path leading from the spring to the hut, speaking as they walked. That night the bird remained in Dai Lao forest. Concealed in the branches of a tree, the bird watched the light of the fire flickering inside the hut, where the two monks conversed through the night.

The bird flew high, high over the ancient forest. For several days it flew back and forth in the sky without landing. Below stood the great tree in the ancient forest; below, the creatures of the mountain and forest were concealed by grass, bushes, and trees. Since the day the bird listened to the exchange between the two monks, its bewilderment grew. Where have I come from and where will I go? How many thousands of years will the great tree stand?

The bird had heard the two monks speak about Time. What is Time? Why has Time brought us here, and why will it take us away? The nut which a bird eats has its own delicious nature. How can I find out the nature of Time? The bird wanted to pick up a small piece of Time and lie quietly with it in its nest for several days to examine its nature. Even if it took months or years to examine, the bird was willing.

The bird flew high, high over the ancient forest. It was like a round balloon drifting in nothingness. The bird felt its nature was as empty as a balloon's. The emptiness of its nature was the ground of its existence, but it was also the cause of the bird's suffering. "Time, if I could find you, certainly I could find myself," thought the bird.

After several days and nights, the bird came to rest quietly in its nest. It had brought back a tiny piece of earth from the Dai Lao forest. Deep in thought, it picked up the piece of earth to examine it. The monk from the Dai Lao forest had said to his friend, "Time is stilled in Eternity. There Love and beloved are One. Each blade of grass, each piece of earth, each leaf, is one with that love."

The bird was still unable to find Time. The small token of earth from the Dai Lao forest revealed nothing. Perhaps the monk lied to his friend. Time lies in Love, where is Love? The bird remembered the splashing waterfalls endlessly tumbling in the Northwest forest. It remembered the days it listened to the sound of the waterfalls from morning to evening. The bird had imagined itself tumbling like a waterfall. It played with the light shining on the water, with the waterfall it caressed the pebbles and rocks in the streams. In those moments, the bird felt that it was a waterfall itself, that the sound of endless falling water came from it.

One noon, flying across the Dai Lao forest, the bird did not see the hut. The whole forest had burned; only a pile of ashes remained where the monk's hut had been. In a panic, the bird flew around searching. The monk was no longer in the forest. Where had he gone? Corpses of animals. Corpses of birds. Had the fire consumed the monk? The bird was bewildered. Time, what are you? Why do you bring us here and why will you take us away? The monk said, "Time is stilled in Eternity." If that is so, perhaps Love has returned the monk to Itself.

Suddenly the bird felt very anxious. It flew swiftly back to the ancient forest. Anguished cries of many birds. Explosions. The ancient forest, far away, was burning. Faster, faster still, the bird flew. The fire licked the sky. The fire spread near the great tree. Hundreds of thousands of birds shrieked in fright.

The fire approached the great tree. The bird fanned the fire with its wings, hoping to put it out, but the fire burned more fiercely. The bird sped to the spring, dipped its wings in the water, and rushed back to shake the water over the forest. The drops sizzled. It was not enough, not enough. The bird's entire body soaked in water was not enough to extinguish the fire.

Cries of hundreds of thousands of birds. Screams of young birds without feathers to fly. The fire began to burn the great tree. Why was there no rain? Why didn't the downpour that fell endlessly in the Northwest forest flow like a waterfall? The bird let forth a piercing cry. The cry was tragic and passionate and was suddenly transformed into the rushing sound of a waterfall. All at once, the bird felt the fullness of its existence. Loneliness and emptiness vanished as an illusion. The image of the monk. The image of the sun behind the mountain peak. The image of rushing water falling endlessly through a thousand lifetimes. The cry of the bird was now the full sound of the waterfall. Without anxiety, the bird plunged into the forest fire like a majestic waterfall.

The next morning was calm. The marvelous rays of the sun shone, but there was no symphony, no voices of tens of thousands of birds. Portions of the forest were completely burned. The great tree still stood, but more than half of its branches and leaves were charred. Corpses of large birds, corpses of small birds. The morning forest was silent.

The birds still alive called one another, their voices bewildered. They did not know by what grace the clear sky had suddenly poured forth rain, extinguishing the forest fire the afternoon before. They remembered seeing the bird shaking water from its two wings. They knew it was the white bird from the great tree. They flew everywhere throughout the forest seeking the corpse of the white bird, but they did not find it.

Perhaps the bird had flown away to live in a different forest. Perhaps the bird had been killed by the fire. The great tree, its body covered with wounds, did not say a word. The birds cocked their heads to the sky and began to build new nests in the wounded body of the great tree. Does the great tree miss the child which sacred mountain air and the life energy of 4,000 years had given birth to? Bird, where have you gone? Listen to the monk: I believe Time has returned the bird to the Love which is the source of all things.